# DON JOHN OF AUSTRIA

ARMS OF DON JOHN OF AUSTRIA
Drawn by Major T. Shepard, F.S.A.

hield party per pale, the dexter side per fess Castile
n, the sinister side per pale Arragon and Arragon-
ver all an escutcheon of pretence Austria impaling
(Ancient).

out of a coronet a bush of peacocks' feathers.

the shield the collar of the Order of the Golden Fleece.

*By the same author :*

ST. FRANCIS XAVIER

*and three novels :*

A KING OF SHADOWS
UNCERTAIN GLORY
SALT

# DON JOHN OF AUSTRIA

## By MARGARET YEO

" There was a man sent from God whose name was John "
(*Inscription on Don John's tomb in the Escorial*)

NEW YORK

SHEED & WARD INC.

MCMXXXIV